Best Easy Day Hikes
Shenandoah National Park

Help Us Keep This Guide Up to Date

Every effort has been made by the authors and editors to make this guide as accurate and useful as possible. However, many things can change after a guide is published—trails are rerouted, regulations change, facilities come under new management, etc.

We would love to hear from you concerning your experiences with this guide and how you feel it could be improved and kept up to date. While we may not be able to respond to all comments and suggestions, we'll take them to heart and we'll also make certain to share them with the authors. Please send your comments and suggestions to the following address:

> The Globe Pequot Press
> Reader Response/Editorial Department
> P.O. Box 480
> Guilford, CT 06437

Or you may e-mail us at:

> editorial@GlobePequot.com

Thanks for your input, and happy trails!

A **FALCON** GUIDE®

Best Easy Day Hikes Series

Best Easy Day Hikes
Shenandoah
National Park

Third Edition
Bert and Jane Gildart

FALCON GUIDES®

GUILFORD, CONNECTICUT
HELENA, MONTANA
AN IMPRINT OF THE GLOBE PEQUOT PRESS

𝐴FALCONGUIDE®

Copyright © 2002, 2006 by Morris Book
Publishing, LLC
A previous edition of this book was published
by Falcon Publishing, Inc. in 1998.

Maps by XNR Productions, Ltd. © Morris
Book Publishing, LLC

ISSN 1541-1044
ISBN 978-0-7627-3415-3

Manufactured in the United States of America
Third Edition/Fifth Printing

Contents

North District

Central District

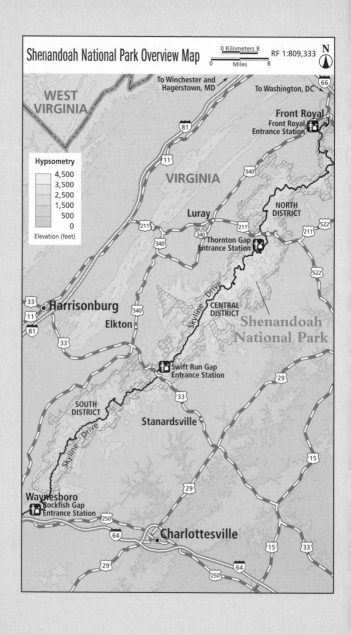

South District

Acknowledgments

No book is ever written and completed without the help of others, and this guide is no exception. First, we'd like to thank the staff at Shenandoah National Park who reviewed the book and provided much valuable information. We attempted to incorporate all their thoughts, suggestions, and ideas and hope we have interpreted their comments correctly. As well, we'd like to thank Karen Michaud at the Interpretation Division and Greta Miller, director of the Shenandoah National Park Association. Both aided with initial logistics and helped us establish just what direction our work would follow.

Along the trails we met the South District Trail Crew, who offered much good trailside chat and helped explain new Shenandoah backcountry policy. Thanks as well to former ranger and adventurer Buck Hisey, now of the Shenandoah Valley, and his wife, Fran (also an adventurer extraordinaire), for their spontaneous friendship, meals, and long night of information about Shenandoah.

Last, but never least, our sincere thanks to Jennifer Quint, Bill Schneider, and Scott Adams of The Globe Pequot Press for their suggestions and continuous help.

Introduction

Shenandoah National Park straddles a beautiful stretch of the Blue Ridge, which forms the eastern rampart of the Appalachian Mountains. Beginning in the late 1700s, settlers began drifting into these hills and "hollers." They cleared some of the vast forests that originally blanketed the region so that they could till the land. Shenandoah was established as a national park in 1935. For the most part, the forests reestablished naturally. As the flora returned, so did Shenandoah's fauna. Today, some 200 species of birds occupy the park, as well as some 50 species of mammals, some of which had declined significantly in number prior to the park's establishment.

Today, Shenandoah offers a little something for everyone with an interest in the out-of-doors. The park attracts more than a million visitors annually and, to accommodate these crowds, is open twenty-four hours a day, seven days a week unless the roads are closed due to ice and/or snow, or fog. Two visitor centers, Dickey Ridge in the North District and Byrd Visitor Center at Big Meadows, are open seven days a week from 8:30 A.M. to 5:00 P.M. beginning about the first of April and usually closing in late November. Loft Mountain Information Center in the South District is open intermittently. For current park information for those who don't have time to write, call headquarters at (540) 999–3500.

As a further means of accommodating visitors, the park has four public campgrounds with a total of 660 campsites. In some of the campgrounds, sites are allocated on a first-come, first-served basis. Getting a spot can be difficult, particularly in the summer and in the fall, when autumn foliage peaks.

At Big Meadows Campground, make reservations for mid-May through October. Even if you arrive during the week, and get a spot, there is some chance you might have to move as the weekend rolls around, because visitors with reservations have priority.

Though Shenandoah offers many attractions, hikes to the waterfalls and highest peaks remain among the most popular. Fortunately, access to these most scenic of attractions is relatively easy.

Getting There

Shenandoah is easily accessible from a variety of different locales. In the north, you can access the park via Front Royal, Virginia, by leaving U.S. Highway 340 south of town and following the bold and abundant signs to the park's entrance. From the highway, the park's northern entrance station is less than a mile away.

From the south, you can access the park by driving from Waynesboro via U.S. Highway 250 to the Rockfish Gap entrance station. You can also enter at its Thornton Gap entrance, 30 miles farther north, via Highway 211. If you are coming through Harrisonburg to the west or Stanardsville to the east, you can enter on Highway 33 at the Swift Run Gap entrance. From Charlottesville and Richmond, you can take Interstate 64 west to Rockfish Gap, the park's southernmost entrance.

Once in the park, you will drive the famous Skyline Drive. Along the west side of this 105.4-mile route, the park has conveniently placed mile markers. Because almost all trails radiate from Skyline Drive, it's very simple to find your desired trailhead. The mileposts begin just after the north entrance of the park, accessed from the town of Front Royal. The last marker, Milepost 105.4, is located at Rockfish Gap in the south. From here, the Blue Ridge Parkway continues south; the town of Waynesboro is at the base of the mountains as you leave the park.

On your road map, you may notice that Skyline Drive does not run precisely north and south. However, for purposes of this guidebook, all directions assume that as you drive from the north end of the park to the south end, east will be on your left and west will be to your right.

What Is a "Best Easy" Hike?

While researching and writing a much larger FalconGuide called *Hiking Shenandoah,* we had frequent discussions with rangers about what kind of information hikers most often requested. We also had the same type of discussion with many hikers on the trails.

It seems there are two general types of visitors—those who want to spend several days exploring Shenandoah's backcountry and those who will be in the park only a day or two and would like a choice sampling of its special features. This book is for the second group.

The more comprehensive book, *Hiking Shenandoah,* covers nearly every trail in the park, including those that are neither best nor easy. *Best Easy Day Hikes* includes only short, less strenuous hikes that we consider among the nicest day hikes in the park. None have drastically long climbs.

Some of the hikes in this book might seem easy to some but not to others. To help you decide which are for you, we have ranked the hikes from easiest to hardest on page 4. Please keep in mind that short does not always equal easy.

Other factors such as elevation gain and trail conditions have to be considered.

We hope you enjoy your "best easy" hiking in Shenandoah National Park.

Ranking the Hikes

The following list ranks the hikes in this book from easiest to hardest. The milepost numbers correspond to those displayed along Skyline Drive and indicate the hike's location on this, the main route through the park.

Limberlost (wheelchair-accessible), Mile 43
Story of the Forest Trail, Mile 51
Fox Hollow Trail, Mile 4.6
Snead Farm, Mile 5.1
Traces Trail, Mile 22.2
Loft Mountain Loop, Mile 79.5
Bettys Rock and Crescent Rock, Mile 44.4
Blackrock Summit, Mile 84.8
Calvary and Chimney Rocks, Mile 90
Calf Mountain, Mile 99.5
Pocosin Trail, Mile 59.5
Millers Head, Mile 42.5
Lands Run Falls, Mile 9.2
Stony Man Trail, Mile 41.7
Byrds Nest 4 Loop, Mile 28.5
Corbin Cabin Cutoff/Nicholson Hollow/AT Loop, Mile 37.9
Marys Rock, Mile 31.6
Hawksbill Summit, Mile 45.6
Bearfence Mountain, Mile 56.4
Rapidan Camp, Mile 52.8

Lewis Spring Falls, Mile 51.2
South River Falls, Mile 62.8
Powell Gap, Mile 69.9
Dark Hollow Falls, Mile 50.7
Ivy Creek, Mile 77.5
Whiteoak Canyon, Mile 45.6

Zero Impact

Visiting a national park such as Shenandoah is like going to a famous art museum. Obviously, you do not want to leave your mark on an art treasure in the museum. If every visitor to the museum left one little mark, the piece of art would quickly be destroyed—and of what value is a big building full of trashed art? The same goes for a wilderness such as Shenandoah National Park, which is as magnificent and as valuable as any masterpiece by any artist. If we all left one little mark on the landscape, the wilderness would soon be despoiled.

A wilderness can accommodate plenty of human use as long as everybody behaves. But a few thoughtless or uninformed visitors can ruin it for everybody who follows. The need for good manners applies to all wilderness users, not just hikers.

Three Falcon Zero-Impact Principles

- Leave with everything you brought in.
- Leave no sign of your visit.
- Leave the landscape as you found it.

Most of us know better than to litter—in or out of the wilderness. Be sure you leave nothing, regardless of how small it is, along the trail or at your campsite. This means that you should pack out everything, including orange peels, flip tops, cigarette butts, and gum wrappers. Also, pick up any trash that others leave behind.

Follow the main trail. Avoid cutting switchbacks and walking on vegetation beside the trail. In the mountains some terrain is very fragile, so stay on the trail if possible.

Don't pick up souvenirs, such as rocks, antlers, or wildflowers. And remember, here in Shenandoah you must go even further. Should you see old bedsprings or other items discarded by the mountain people of yesteryear, leave them as you found them. Park officials regard them as historic artifacts.

Avoid making loud noises that may disturb others. Remember, sound travels easily along the ridges and through the canyons. Be courteous.

Bury human waste 6 to 8 inches deep and pack out used toilet paper. This is a good reason to carry a lightweight trowel. Keep waste at least 300 feet away from any water source.

Finally, and perhaps most importantly, strictly follow the pack-in and pack-out rule. If you carry something into the backcountry, consume it or carry it out.

About the Maps

The maps in this book use elevation tints called hypsometry, to portray relief. Each gray tone represents a range of equal elevation, as shown in the scale key with the map. The darker tones are lower elevations and the lighter grays are higher elevations. Narrow bands of different gray tones spaced closely together indicate steep terrain, whereas wider bands indicate areas of more gradual slope.

Map Legend

Boundaries

National park boundary

Other national land boundary

Transportation

Interstate highway   40

U.S. highway   89

State highway   64

Other highway   18 610

Primary/other roads

Unpaved road

Unimproved road

Featured trail

Shared trail

Other trail

Unverified trail

Hydrology

River

Creek

Intermittent stream

Spring

Falls/rapids

Lake

Sand

Physiography

Cave

Cliff

Pass

Peak/elevation   ▲+ Dickey Hill 2,444 ft.

Symbols

Backcountry campsite

Bridge

Cabin/shelter

Campground

Gate

Turnaround

Parking

Picnic area

Point of interest

Ranger station

Restroom

Ruin

Town

Trailhead

Visitor center

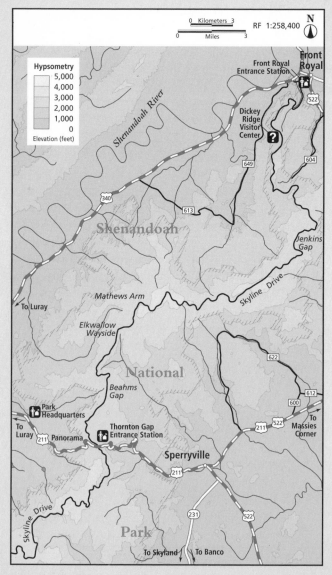

1 Fox Hollow Trail

Start: Dickey Ridge Visitor Center, Skyline Mile 4.6.
Type of hike: Loop.
Distance: 1.2 miles.
Approximate hiking time: 30 to 60 minutes.

Elevation gain and loss: 310 feet.
Maps: National Geographic Trails Illustrated Topo Map 228; Map 9, Appalachian Trail and other trails in Shenandoah National Park, North District (PATC, Inc.).

The Hike

Begin the hike on the east side of Skyline Drive, across from the Dickey Ridge Visitor Center. The kiosk provides further information about the area and serves as the trailhead. The trail begins with a slight descent and soon accesses Dickey Ridge Trail to the left. Turn left and follow that blue-blazed trail for 0.2 mile, and then turn right onto Fox Hollow Trail, also blue-blazed, past piles of rocks reflecting the work once required to clear the forest and prepare it for cultivation.

The trail continues to descend gradually, passing a spring and a mill wheel once used for ornamental purposes. At 0.5 mile, the trail passes the Fox family cemetery. The largest stone memorializes Lemuel F. Fox, the son of Thomas Fox, who established the family farm here in 1856. According to the inscription, Lemuel died May 24, 1916, at the age of seventy-eight. The trail continues to cross old farmland now being reclaimed by the forest. Deer have returned to the area and now abound.

Shortly after passing the cemetery, the trail begins its return to the visitor center by climbing gradually. Along the trail, rock piles and rock fences continue to proclaim that

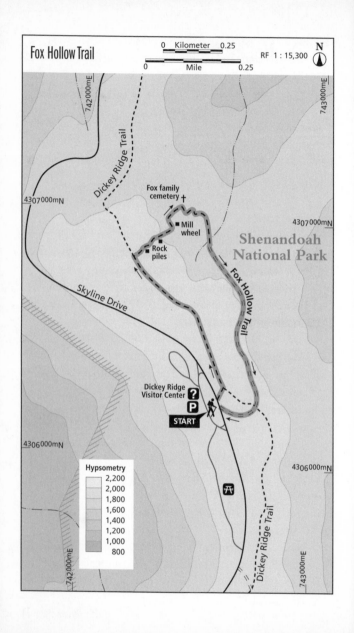

farming once dominated the area. The path is actually an old road that once linked the Fox family with the town of Front Royal.

Pets are not allowed on this trail.

Miles and Directions

0.0 Park kiosk on east side of Skyline Drive, at Dickey Ridge Visitor Center.

0.15 Cement post. Turn left onto blue-blazed Dickey Ridge Trail.

0.3 Cement post. Take right fork east onto blue-blazed Fox Hollow Trail.

0.35 First of many rock piles.

0.5 Fox Farm Cemetery. Continue south on Fox Hollow Trail.

1.1 Shortly after mile 1.1, you'll encounter a cement post marking the Dickey Ridge Trail (blue-blazed) going north/south. Do not turn; stay straight.

1.2 You're back at the trailhead.

2 Snead Farm

Start: Skyline Mile 5.1 on Skyline Drive. This trail can be accessed at the end of Fox Hollow Trail by turning left onto Dickey Ridge Trail. Or cross Skyline Drive to the east, opposite the exit for the Dickey Ridge picnic area. You can park either at the visitor center or at the south end of the picnic grounds.
Type of hike: Out and back or loop.

Distance: 1.4 miles or 3.2 miles.
Approximate hiking time: 1 to 2 hours.
Elevation gain and loss: 500 feet.
Maps: National Geographic Trails Illustrated Topo Map 228; Map 9, Appalachian Trail and other trails in Shenandoah National Park, North District (PATC, Inc.).

The Hike

The visit to Snead Farm is a trip back in time. Once the owners worked this 200-acre piece of land as farmland and as an apple orchard. The park bought the land in 1962. The remnants here are quite visible; the barn still stands, as does the root cellar. The stone remains of an old house fill an open area. With but little imagination, you can recognize the difficulty these people had in clearing and farming this land.

After accessing Snead Farm Road, bear left at the first fork, right at the second fork, and left at the last fork. The walk to the farm is a pleasant one along an old farm road. Upon reaching the farm, take time to explore the barn. Peer into the old root cellar; examine the stone foundation of the bunkhouse.

From Snead Farm, you can retrace your steps to the picnic area for an out-and-back hike of 1.4 miles. Or you can

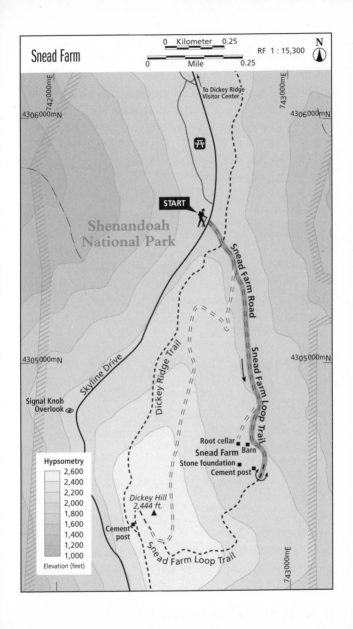

Snead Farm

0   Kilometer   0.25

0   Mile   0.25

RF 1 : 15,300

N

To Dickey Ridge
Visitor Center

4306000mN

742000mE

743000mE

4306000mN

START

Shenandoah
National Park

Snead Farm Road

4305000mN

Skyline Drive

Dickey Ridge Trail

Snead Farm Loop Trail

4305000mN

Signal Knob
Overlook

Root cellar

Snead Farm   Barn

Stone foundation

Cement post

Dickey Hill
2,444 ft.

Cement
post

Snead Farm Loop Trail

Hypsometry

2,600
2,400
2,200
2,000
1,800
1,600
1,400
1,200
1,000

Elevation (feet)

743000mE

make it a 3.2-mile loop hike by accessing the blue-blazed Snead Farm Loop Trail, which begins at a cement post near the stone foundation at mile 0.9.

Hike about 1 mile to another cement post at a T-junction with the Dickey Ridge Trail. Go north (right) onto Dickey Ridge Trail. The visitor center is 1.3 miles from this point.

The trail begins a slightly strenuous ascent to the top of Dickey Hill. At the summit, take the spur trail to your right. For a marvelous view of Signal Knob on Massanutten Mountain and of the Shenandoah Valley, go left. A hang glider launch area is located just before the path to the viewpoint.

Back on Dickey Ridge Trail, you will make another quick ascent. Then the trail begins to descend gradually beneath a canopy of trees. It continues through a quiet woods to an intersection with Skyline Drive near the picnic area, completing the loop.

Miles and Directions

0.0   Chain gate across drive from picnic area. Stay on Snead Farm Road.

0.1   Fork in road; stay left.

0.3   Fork in road; stay right.

0.5   Fork in road; stay left.

0.7   Remains of Snead Farm. Retrace your steps from here for a hike of 1.4 miles.

Or:

For a loop hike of 3.2 miles:

0.9   Access the Snead Farm Loop Trail from the cement post opposite the stone foundation. Follow this trail south (to your right as you face the post) to another cement post.

1.9 At cement post, turn right (north) onto the blue-blazed Dickey Ridge Trail.

3.2 Trailhead, end of loop.

3 Lands Run Falls

Start: Lands Run parking area, Skyline Mile 9.2.
Type of hike: Out and back.
Distance: 1.2 miles.
Approximate hiking time: 30 to 60 minutes.

Elevation gain and loss: About 300 feet.
Maps: National Geographic Trails Illustrated Topo Map 228; Map 9, Appalachian Trail and other trails in Shenandoah National Park, North District (PATC Inc.).

The Hike

Lands Run Falls is not especially high, nor can you see the entire falls from the trail. But the setting is lovely, and the trek provides a nice leg stretcher. Woods flanking the trail are dominated by oaks and hickories, interspersed with tulip poplars. Many of the healthiest oaks here were knocked down by Tropical Storm Fran in 1996. Those not already denuded by gypsy moths were so heavily laden with leaves that they were easily toppled by the strong winds. In addition to a lovely forest, there is a great deal of greenstone (volcanic rock) exposed by soil erosion. Look for greenstone on the uphill side of the road.

Follow the fire road, which descends immediately and continues to do so for 0.6 mile. At that point, a stream courses down the hill from the left and passes through a culvert under the road. The falls are on the right. By taking a

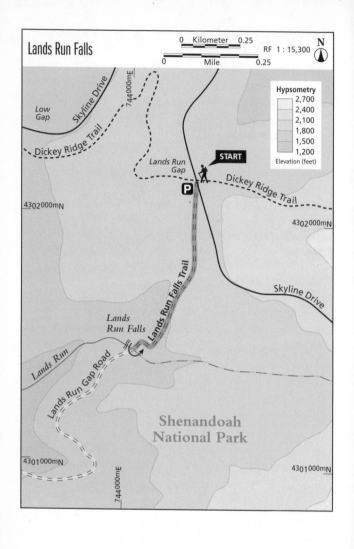

short spur trail to the right, you can get some inspiring views. The slick rocks and precipitous grade create a potential hazard, so use caution.

The road continues for another 1.4 miles to the park boundary. Unless you have lots of energy to burn, there is not much point in continuing the hike; the road descends another 600 feet with no viewpoints. Retrace your steps from the falls—uphill, of course, including one short, steep portion.

Miles and Directions

0.0 Fire road at south end of Lands Run parking area, Mile 9.2.

0.6 Stream entering from left; waterfall on right. Retrace your steps back.

1.2 Lands Run parking area.

4 Traces Trail

Start: East end of amphitheater parking lot, Mathews Arm Campground, Skyline Mile 22.2.
Type of hike: Loop.
Distance: 1.7 miles.
Approximate hiking time: 1 to 3 hours, depending on your degree of fascination with cultural and natural history.

Elevation gain and loss: Negligible.
Maps: National Geographic Trails Illustrated Topo Map 228; Map 9, Appalachian Trail and other trails in Shenandoah National Park, North District (PATC, Inc.).

The Hike

Packing much into a short distance, this is a great hike for families with small children as well as for people who no longer hike as well as they once did. It should also appeal to anyone who has an interest in natural and cultural history. The trail is ideally located for the RV camper, since it departs from Mathews Arm Campground. Dogs are prohibited from this trail.

Along the trail, you will see a lot of greenstone, a type of volcanic rock that was formed 800 million years ago.

The deer exclosure was constructed in 1993, and you may be able to guess its purpose—particularly if you have hiked other park trails and seen many deer. In the mid-1930s heavy hunting almost decimated the deer population. Since then it has bounced back to the point that some wildlife experts fear the animals may be exceeding the capacity of their range. The exclosure will enable managers to compare areas that cannot be grazed by deer with those that can, to determine whether the grazing is harming the environment.

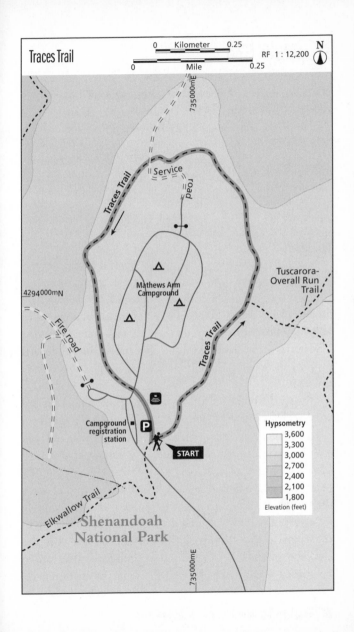

If so, the park may consider implementing some form of deer management.

Access the trailhead from the east end of the parking lot, which serves the amphitheater to the right of the entrance station. The trail is broad and begins beneath a mantle of red oak. Soon the trail climbs above the amphitheater. If the trail is wet, it may be slippery, so use caution. Toward the end of your hike, there is a huge oak that for some reason was spared the ax. If trees could speak, this one could probably relate close to 200 years of history.

Near trail's end, the forest canopy opens slightly, offering hints of other, more lofty vistas. After a 1.7-mile hike, return via the trail to the west end of the parking lot.

Because the trail climbs so gently, you can probably complete this hike in an hour—if an hour is all the time you have.

Miles and Directions

0.0 Sign at east end of amphitheater.
0.4 Cement post at sign 9. Stay left; descend.
1.0 Cement post at sign 17. Go straight.
1.7 Amphitheater parking lot.

5 Byrds Nest Summit and Byrds Nest Shelter No. 4

Start: Beahms Gap parking area, Skyline Mile 28.5.
Type of hike: Out and back.
Distance: 3.2 miles.
Approximate hiking time: 2 hours.
Elevation gain and loss: About 490 feet.

Maps: National Geographic Trails Illustrated Topo Map 228; Map 9, Appalachian Trail and other trails in Shenandoah National Park, North District (PATC, Inc.).

The Hike

This short, relatively easy day hike takes you up to a ridge on the Neighbor Mountain Trail and to the Byrds Nest Shelter No. 4, a day-use shelter built in 1965. It is one of four shelters in the park constructed with donations from former Sen. Harry F. Byrd Sr. The trek is pretty and tranquil. On clear days you can see beyond Pass Mountain to the east. The shelter is a large, three-sided stone structure with a huge fireplace and picnic table.

Begin this hike at the cement post at the north end of the parking lot. Descend 0.1 mile through the woods to a T junction at another cement post. Here the Appalachian Trail runs north/south. Turn north (right) onto the AT. Soon you'll encounter a cement post indicating a spring on the left.

As you trek through a mostly deciduous forest (pretty in the fall), the trees and rocks offset one another's beauty. There are a few short, steep ascents and a few very rocky

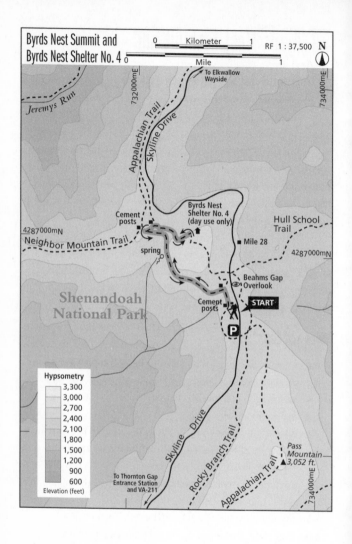

areas of trail. Sturdy boots are recommended, especially if the trail is wet.

At 1 mile, you'll encounter a four-way junction of the AT and the Neighbor Mountain Trail. Turn east (right) onto the Neighbor Mountain Trail. In 0.1 mile, another post is encountered. Here, stay straight on the Neighbor Mountain Trail for 0.5 mile more to Byrds Nest Shelter No. 4.

You'll find the shelter in a pretty setting, one that inspires a picnic. A field lies in front of you, and flowers give color in summer. Pass Mountain rises to the east. If you wander to the right above the shelter, it may be possible to get some views, but nothing outstanding. From here, you'll need to retrace your route to the parking lot. You will note that in the first 0.6 mile of the return trip, at the cement posts, you are able to take a short spur trail down to Skyline Drive. If you do make this choice, be aware that you will come out north of where you left your vehicle at Beahms Gap.

Miles and Directions

0.0 Cement post, north end of parking lot at Beahms Gap.

0.1 Cement post and junction with the Appalachian Trail. Turn north (right) onto the AT.

0.2 Spring on left; stay on AT.

1.0 Byrds Nest Summit. Four-way cement post with junction with AT and Neighbor Mountain Trail. Turn right onto the Neighbor Mountain Trail.

1.1 Another cement post; stay straight on Neighbor Mountain Trail.

1.5 Cement post; stay straight on Neighbor Mountain Trail.

1.6 Byrds Nest Shelter No. 4. Retrace your steps.

3.2 Beahms Gap parking lot.

CENTRAL DISTRICT OVERVIEW

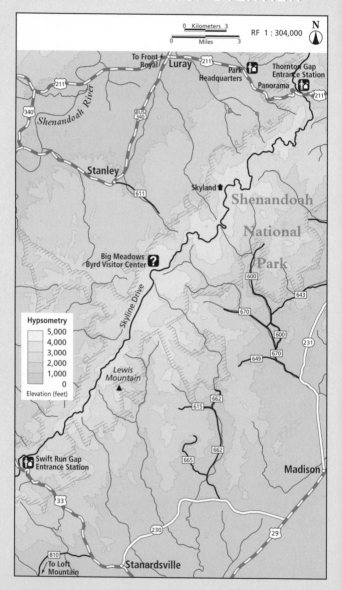

6 Marys Rock

Start: Upper parking lot at Panorama, Skyline Mile 31.6, near Thornton Gap Entrance Station.

Type of hike: Out and back.

Distance: 3.6 miles.

Approximate hiking time: 2 to 4 hours.

Elevation gain and loss: 1,210 feet.

Maps: National Geographic Trails Illustrated Topo Map 228; Map 10, Appalachian Trail and other trails in Shenandoah National Park, Central District (PATC, Inc.).

The Hike

If you have the luxury of time, pick a clear day for this hike and go early in the morning. Sunrise is a great time to enjoy the views and get some superb photos. (Save foggy days for hikes to waterfalls; fog adds to the aura of wetness.)

According to one version of park lore, a young woman named Mary Thornton once made this hike alone to the rocky summit. When she returned, she carried a bear cub under each arm. The park certainly does not endorse such intimacy with wildlife today, but the story is a good one.

To begin the trek, head left (south) on the Appalachian Trail, which is marked with white blazes. Within 30 yards, the trail begins to climb. Twelve log steps help you upward. Within 100 yards, five more log steps do the same thing. The trail winds upward through a hardwood forest interspersed with mountain laurel and ferns. It follows the east side of the ridge. Soon the trees are more widely spaced and views begin. The trail becomes very rocky and is fortified on your left with a man-made shelf of rocks. On the upward slope, the trees seem to be trying to restrain the

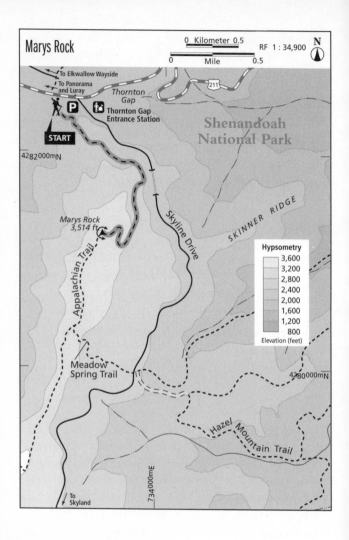

Marys Rock

0 Kilometer 0.5

0 Mile 0.5

RF 1 : 34,900

N

To Elkwallow Wayside

To Panorama and Luray

211

Thornton Gap

P

Thornton Gap Entrance Station

START

Shenandoah National Park

4282000mN

Marys Rock 3,514 ft

Appalachian Trail

Skyline Drive

SKINNER RIDGE

Hypsometry

3,600
3,200
2,800
2,400
2,000
1,600
1,200
800
Elevation (feet)

Meadow Spring Trail

4280000mN

Hazel Mountain Trail

734000mE

To Skyland

force of gravity, preventing large boulders from tumbling down the hillside. The ascent is steady, with some switch-backs and few level areas.

After about a mile, there are large rock monoliths to your right and a lovely panorama to the east. As you approach the summit, the trail swings back into the trees. On the uphill side of the trail, thick stands of mountain laurel line the path. At our approach, a ruffed grouse took wing.

You will encounter your first cement post after 1.7 miles. Do not continue on the AT, which veers left. Keep going straight ahead, taking the spur trail to the top, which is 0.1 mile farther. Be sure to follow the blue blazes, not the white ones along the AT.

Marys Rock is composed of Pedlar granodiorite. The vista below is wonderful; you can see Thornton Gap. Plan to spend some time here resting in the clearing or carefully climbing the rocks for different views. You might see pere-grine falcons soaring on the wind drafts, as we did.

Now that you have climbed 1,210 feet to the top, you can enjoy the luxury of a downhill return. Backtrack, taking the AT north, but use caution: The steep, rocky descent can be more hazardous than the uphill trek, especially when wet.

Miles and Directions

0.0   Cement post at end of upper parking lot at Panorama.

0.1   Junction with Appalachian Trail; turn left.

1.0   Large rock monoliths on right.

1.7   Cement post. Go straight on spur trail. Do not turn left on AT.

1.8   Summit of Marys Rock. Retrace your steps.

3.6   Upper parking lot at Panorama.

7 Corbin Cabin Cutoff/Nicholson Hollow/AT Loop

Start: Cement post on east side of Skyline Drive at Mile 37.9.
Type of hike: Out and back or loop.
Distance: 2.9 miles or 4.3 miles.
Approximate hiking time: 3 to 4 hours.

Elevation gain and loss: 1,095 feet or 1,350 feet.
Maps: National Geographic Trails Illustrated Topo Map 228; Map 10, Appalachian Trail and other trails in Shenandoah National Park, Central District (PATC, Inc.).

The Hike

On this hike, head downhill via the Corbin Cabin Cutoff Trail, ascend via the Nicholson Hollow Trail, and end up on the other side of Skyline Drive by way of the Appalachian Trail. The route passes "Freestate" Hollow (named by the Nicholson clan) and an abandoned cabin. Visiting a cabin such as this provides a glimpse of what life may have been like for the men, women, and children who once lived in the hollows.

Appropriately, the hike begins by descending a trail built by the mountain people who once inhabited the area. Begin at the trailhead on the east side of Skyline Drive and drop gradually for about 25 yards to a cement post that identifies the 1.4-mile hike to Corbin Cabin.

As the steep and rocky trail continues to drop, it is flanked on either side by lush stands of mountain laurel. After about half a mile, it turns to the right in a southeasterly direction. To your east is a small, dry streambed. Shortly thereafter, the

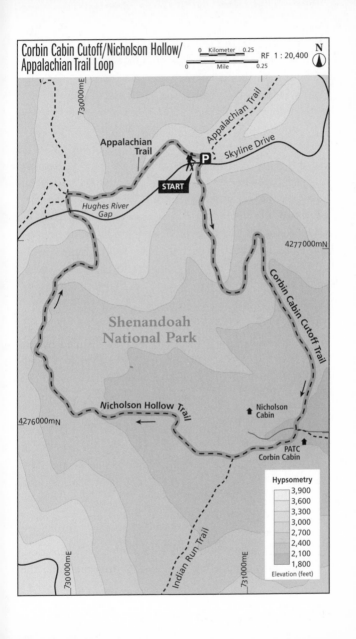

Corbin Cabin Cutoff/Nicholson Hollow/ Appalachian Trail Loop

0   Kilometer   0.25

0   Mile   0.25

RF 1 : 20,400

N

730000mE

Appalachian Trail

Appalachian Trail

Skyline Drive

P

START

Hughes River Gap

4277000mN

Corbin Cabin Cutoff Trail

Shenandoah National Park

Nicholson Cabin

Nicholson Hollow Trail

4276000mN

PATC Corbin Cabin

Indian Run Trail

730000mE

731000mE

Hypsometry

	3,900
	3,600
	3,300
	3,000
	2,700
	2,400
	2,100
	1,800

Elevation (feet)

trail levels and begins to climb gradually.

About 0.9 mile from the trailhead are the first clear remnants of early human activity. Jumbles of rocks flank the right side of the trail, and to the left, downhill, are the ruins of the John R. Nicholson Cabin. The flowing stream below it has a nice pool.

Continue on the trail and rock-hop across the Hughes River to Corbin Cabin. Just before the river is a cabin that once belonged to Albert and Mamie Nicholson. It is hidden in the trees to the right of the trail. This one is fairly intact, allowing you to get an idea of how it was constructed.

Corbin Cabin is in front of you as you cross the river. The Potomac Appalachian Trail Club (PATC) renovated the cabin in 1954 and now rents it to hikers. The spot is idyllic, and you may want to have a picnic in the yard, if no one is currently renting.

From here, you must make a choice. Do you retrace your steps, for a hike of 2.9 miles, or do you return via the somewhat steep Nicholson Hollow Trail and add another 1.4 miles to your route?

If you choose to continue on the loop hike, take the old mountain road that leads west from Corbin Cabin. This is the Nicholson Hollow Trail, which ascends (steeply in places) to Skyline Drive. The first part of the trail is extremely rough and rocky as it crosses Indian Run (often dry) and climbs through the forest. More than a mile from the cabin, there is a walled-in spring on the left side of the trail, but it is usually dry.

The upper portion of Nicholson Hollow Trail is a fairly straight climb to Skyline Drive. The path is flanked by mountain laurel and oak.

Upon reaching the drive, turn left and walk south for about 75 yards. Cross the drive to your right at an opening in the trees and continue straight ahead to access the AT at a cement post. Turn north (right) onto the AT. Follow it as it winds up and down until you reach the parking area, thus completing this scenic loop hike.

Miles and Directions

- **0.0** Cement post on east side of Skyline Drive, Mile 37.9.
- **0.5** Corbin Cabin Cutoff Trail goes left, then right to parallel a streambed.
- **0.9** Stone wall on right; John T. Nicholson cabin ruins downhill to left.
- **1.4** Albert and Mamie Nicholson cabin in woods to right of trail.
- **1.45** Hughes River crossing; cement post below Corbin cabin. Turnaround point for out and back.
- **1.58** Junction with Indian Run Trail; keep straight.
- **1.8** Indian Run stream crossing (often dry).
- **2.9** Enclosed spring on left.
- **3.8** Skyline Drive. Turn south onto drive; cross drive to cement post. Turn north (right) onto Appalachian Trail.
- **4.3** Return to trailhead.

8 Stony Man Trail

Start: Cement post just inside
Stony Man parking lot, at north
entrance to Skyland, Skyline Mile
41.7.
Type of hike: Out and back.
Distance: 1.4 miles.
Approximate hiking time: 1 to 2
hours.

Elevation gain and loss: 350
feet.
Maps: National Geographic Trails
Illustrated Topo Map 228; Map
10, Appalachian Trail and other
trails in Shenandoah National
Park, Central District (PATC, Inc.).

The Hike

At 4,011 feet, Stony Man is the park's second highest mountain after Hawksbill. The park provides a brochure (nominal fee) with twenty interpretive site descriptions for this self-guided hike.

From the Stony Man parking area inside Skyland, access the Appalachian Trail at the cement post. Follow the trail north (right) for 0.4 mile. Here, the AT reaches its highest point in Shenandoah. At this point, a trail branches off to the west (left) from the AT at a cement post. Follow the trail for 0.1 mile to a split in the trail. Either fork will take you to the summit because the two actually meet to form a loop. At the summit, take time, particularly in the spring, to search the sky for falcons. Over the years, the National Park Service has sponsored a peregrine falcon reintroduction program intended to restore the nation's fastest diving bird to its wild or native range.

To complete the hike, continue around the loop and back to the AT. You are on familiar ground now, so return the way you came.

Pets are not allowed on this trail.

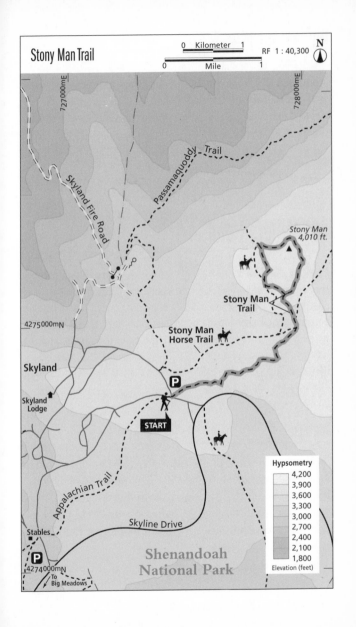

Miles and Directions

0.0 From trailhead, take Appalachian Trail north.

0.4 Junction at cement post with Stony Man Trail; go straight on blue-blazed trail.

0.5 Fork in trail; right or left forms loop to viewpoint.

0.7 Summit of Stony Man, cement post, and junction.

1.0 Cement post and junction with AT. Head straight south on AT.

1.4 Stony Man parking lot.

9 Millers Head

Start: Skyline Mile 42.5 at south entrance to Skyland. Pass stables, take left fork in road, and park at the next gravel road on your left.
Type of hike: Out and back.
Distance: 1.6 miles.
Approximate hiking time: 1.5 hours.

Elevation gain and loss: 475 feet.
Maps: National Geographic Trails Illustrated Topo Map 228; Map 10, Appalachian Trail and other trails in Shenandoah National Park, Central District (PATC, Inc.).

The Hike

Begin your hike in one of two ways: Walk up the gravel road from your car for 0.2 mile to the Millers Head Trail, on the left, or walk up the paved road to the cement post. Either way takes you to the top of Bushytop Mountain. There you will see some large microwave dishes, part of the Skyland communication system.

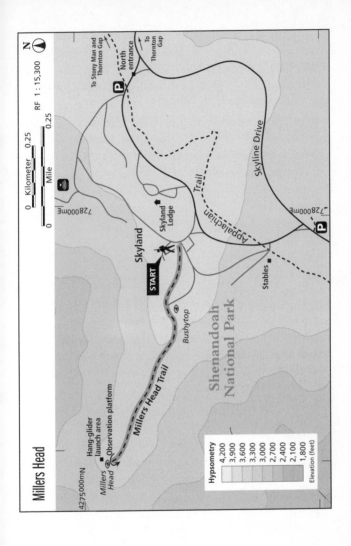

Millers Head

RF 1 : 15,300

0 Kilometer 0.25

0 Mile 0.25

N

To Stony Man and Thornton Gap

North entrance

To Thornton Gap

P

Skyline Drive

Appalachian Trail

728000mE

Skyland

Skyland Lodge

START

Bushytop

Millers Head Trail

Hang-glider launch area

Observation platform

Millers Head

4275000mN

Shenandoah National Park

Stables

P

_728000mE

Hypsometry

4,200
3,900
3,600
3,300
3,000
2,700
2,400
2,100
1,800

Elevation (feet)

Once on Millers Head Trail, head downhill via a series of switchbacks. About 0.3 mile before the observation platform, there is a cement post. Keep going down the trail to the platform. Along the way there are some good views, but none are as nice as the one from the Millers Head observation platform, at an elevation of about 3,460 feet. From here you can get full views of the Page Valley, the town of Luray, Massanutten Mountain, Stony Man, Hawksbill, and Marys and Bettys Rocks. Below the platform is a hang-glider launch site.

This pretty hike is convenient for the many folks who stay at Skyland during their visit to the park.

Miles and Directions

0.0 Trailhead at cement post, 75 yards uphill from parking area.

0.2 Summit of Bushytop. Begin descent on Millers Head Trail.

0.5 Cement post. Head downhill to observation platform.

0.8 Observation platform on Millers Head. Retrace steps.

1.6 Back at trailhead.

10 Limberlost

Start: Mile 43 on Skyline Drive. Turn east at the Limberlost Trail sign and park in the Limberlost parking lot.
Type of hike: Loop.
Distance: 1.3 miles.
Approximate hiking time: 1 hour.

Elevation gain and loss: 100 feet.
Maps: National Geographic Trails Illustrated Topo Map 228; Map 10, Appalachian Trail and other trails in Shenandoah National Park, Central District (PATC, Inc.).

The Hike

Limberlost Trail is ADA accessible, the only such trail in the park. Once lined by ancient hemlocks, it can provide inspiration for all.

Addie Pollock laid the groundwork for preserving the Limberlost Forest. About 1920, she bought one hundred of the largest trees in the area for $1,000. Her husband, George, who established Skyland, named the remnant forest after the Gene Stratton Porter novel *Girl of the Limberlost,* though in that case "limberlost" referred to a fictitious setting in North Carolina.

Here in Shenandoah, the Limberlost Forest also preserves some of the park's oldest and largest red spruce trees. This species is a remnant from the last ice age, and one such tree is believed to be more than 250 years old. This patriarch stands alone by a small stream that you will encounter along the walk.

Because the Limberlost has been designated an Outstanding Natural Area, no bicycles, pets, or camping is

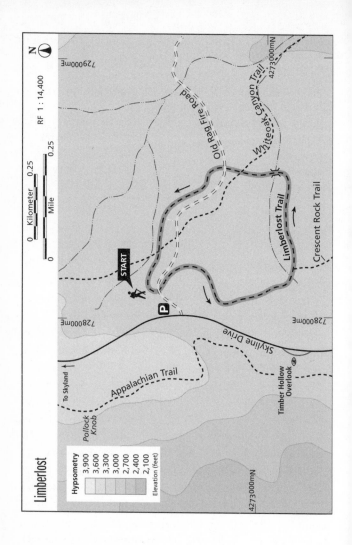

allowed along the trail. The newly reconstructed trail was officially dedicated in the summer of 1997.

After parking, read the information on the trailhead sign and the cement post. Note that other trails radiate from and cross the Limberlost Trail. We chose to hike the path counterclockwise for the following description.

The nearly level path is lined with mountain laurel. Until recently, it was also rimmed by ancient hemlock trees, some said to be 400 years old. Sadly, the exotic insect pest known as the wooly adelgid, which sucks the stored food from the hemlock needles, has wreaked havoc on Limberlost's hemlocks. Now most are gone, dead, having either fallen or been cut down for safety. The trees will lie in place, gradually decaying into the soil. A different plant life form will begin to arise now that the sun can reach the forest floor.

The oak trees in Limberlost have also suffered greatly due to gypsy moth invasions. However, wildflowers bloom in spring and summer; and white pine, birch, and maple trees still flourish in this beautiful place. Limberlost is truly "The Story of a Changing Forest."

As you meander through what was once an old meadow, notice the abundance of wood benches for resting and observing. There is a bench about every 400 feet. Cross a boardwalk over a wet, swampy area; after 0.4 mile, you'll encounter a cement post indicating that at this point, Crescent Rock Trail enters the Limberlost Trail from the south at Skyline Drive. The Limberlost Trail proceeds straight ahead and offers yet another lesson in the devastating power of nature. In the fall of 1996, Tropical Storm Fran swept through the area, uprooting many mature trees and causing extensive trail erosion, which was repaired in 1997 after several months of work.

At 0.7 mile, cross a large wooden bridge. A sign notes, THIS BRIDGE WAS BUILT IN PARTNERSHIP WITH THE BELL ATLANTIC PIONEERS VIRGINIA OLD DOMINION CHAPTER 43. Another cement post points the way to the Whiteoak Canyon Trail access.

Near trail's end, another cement post shows the Whiteoak Canyon Trail going left and right. Stay on the crushed greenstone trail with the Limberlost markers to trail's end and back to the parking lot.

Pets are not allowed on this trail.

Miles and Directions

- **0.0** Trailhead 50 yards from Skyline Drive.
- **0.4** Cement post; junction with Crescent Rock Trail. Stay on Limberlost Trail.
- **0.7** Cross wooden bridge.
- **1.0** Cross myriad other trails. Stay on Limberlost Trail.
- **1.3** Trailhead.

11 Bettys Rock and Crescent Rock

Start: Crescent Rock Overlook at Skyline Mile 44.4. Drive to interpretive sign at center.
Type of hike: Two short, out-and-back strolls.
Distance: Bettys Rock, 550 yards; Crescent Rock, 100 yards.
Approximate hiking time: 15 minutes each.

Elevation gain and loss: Bettys Rock, 100 feet; Crescent Rock, negligible.
Maps: National Geographic Trails Illustrated Topo Map 228; Map 10, Appalachian Trail and other trails in Shenandoah National Park, Central District (PATC, Inc.).

The Hikes

Both of these short, enjoyable jaunts offer spectacular views to the west of the surrounding mountains and the Shenandoah Valley. Both also offer a brief chance to stretch your legs after following long lines of traffic. On wet days, the rocks on the overlooks can be slick, so watch your children and your footing. In places, the rocks drop off suddenly and you should exercise caution.

On the way up to Bettys Rock, alder, oak, and maple trees line the trail. If you hike in the early morning or late afternoon, you may see many deer. From the overlook, look for Hawksbill Mountain to the immediate left. Naked Top is not far from Hawksbill. The Massanutten Range towers across the Shenandoah Valley.

The view is much the same from Crescent Rock. However, the hike is 450 yards shorter.

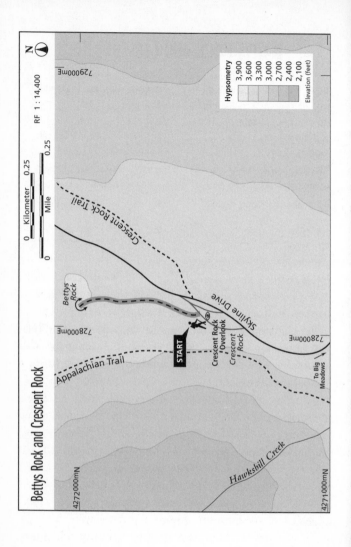

Bettys Rock and Crescent Rock

N

RF 1 : 14,400

0   Kilometer   0.25

0   Mile   0.25

Hypsometry
3,900
3,600
3,300
3,000
2,700
2,400
2,100
Elevation (feet)

729000mE

728000mE

728000mE

4272000mN

4271000mN

Bettys Rock

Crescent Rock Trail

Appalachian Trail

Skyline Drive

START

Crescent Rock Overlook

Crescent Rock

To Big Meadows

Hawksbill Creek

12 Hawksbill Summit

Start: Hawksbill Gap parking area at Mile 45.6 on Skyline Drive. Access trailhead at north end of lot.
Type of hike: Loop.
Distance: 2.8 miles.
Approximate hiking time: 2 to 3 hours.

Elevation gain and loss: About 800 feet.
Maps: National Geographic Trails Illustrated Topo Map 228; Map 10, Appalachian Trail and other trails in Shenandoah National Park, Central District (PATC, Inc.).

The Hike

The trail begins at the north end of Hawksbill Gap parking lot at Mile 45.6 on Skyline Drive. A level spur trail about 100 yards long leads to the Appalachian Trail, which is marked with white blazes. Turn south (left) onto the AT and begin climbing. The trail is rocky and, as always, good hiking boots are recommended. Within 0.4 mile, the trail approaches a rock slide. After another 25 yards, it passes a second talus slope, and there is a view of mountains and valleys spilling off to the west. Half a mile from the trailhead, the trail approaches yet another rock-strewn outcropping, suggestive once again of the erosion of the park's mountains. Lichen cover the rocks, and here and there trees struggle for a foothold in soils that were formed relatively recently.

Toward the summit, foxtail blooms in great abundance; columbine also appears, as does a species of wild geranium. Several rock outcrops tilt upward, revealing layers that look like a stack of pancakes. The area is one of outstanding natural splendor.

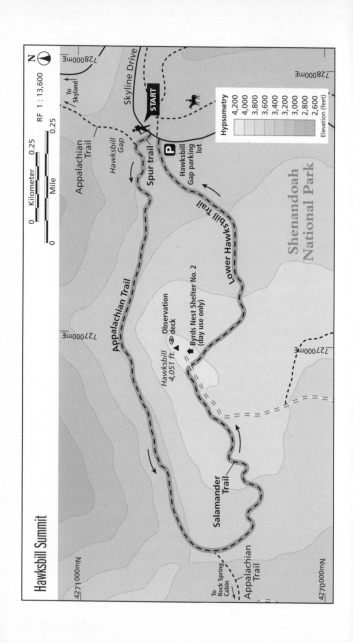

Hawksbill Summit

N

0 Kilometer 0.25

0 Mile 0.25

RF 1 : 13,600

Appalachian Trail

To Skyland

Skyline Drive

START

Hawksbill Gap

Spur trail

P

Hawksbill Gap parking lot

Lower Hawksbill Trail

Shenandoah National Park

Appalachian Trail

Observation deck

Byrds Nest Shelter No. 2 (day use only)

Hawksbill 4,051 ft.

Salamander Trail

To Rock Spring Cabin

Appalachian Trail

728000mE

728000mE

727000mE

727000mE

4271000mN

4270000mN

Hypsometry	
	4,200
	4,000
	3,800
	3,600
	3,400
	3,200
	3,000
	2,800
	2,600

Elevation (feet)

About a mile along the trail, you will come to a cement post noting the mileage along the AT and the distance to Rock Spring Cabin. The post points toward Hawksbill and back toward Fishers Gap. Make a hard left turn onto the Salamander Trail at this point and continue climbing. The summit is only 0.9 mile away. Within a quarter mile of the junction, the rocks covering the trail become more exposed, probably the result of tremendous spring runoff. Near the top, the trail joins a fire road. Keep climbing to the summit, which is not far away. At the summit, there is a shelter named Byrds Nest. The three-sided structure was built with funds provided by former U.S. senator and Virginia governor Harry F. Byrd Sr.; it is one of four such shelters in the park. No water is available at the site, and camping is not permitted on or near the summit.

The shelter is surrounded by red spruce, balsam fir, and mountain ash. Continue the last few yards to the observation platform, and the highest point in the park.

At 4,051 feet, Hawksbill is the park's highest peak, making it an ideal place for birds. Look for the endangered peregrine falcon (*Falco peregrinus*), which has been recorded at Hawksbill and several other surrounding mountains. Peregrines are the nation's swiftest avian species, capable of diving at speeds up to 120 miles an hour.

The view from the top of Hawksbill is commanding and panoramic. Mountains roll off in all directions, blending gradually into yet more mountains in the hazy distance. The Park Service has placed a huge compass at the overlook to help those with maps orient themselves. Stony Man, with its jagged features, is to the north; Browns Mountain spreads neatly to the west. To the south is Graves Mountain. Just below, Skyline Drive threads through the hardwood forest. The town of Luray is to the northwest.

To return to Hawksbill Gap from the summit, retrace your steps to the shelter and go left on the fire road to a cement post. Turn left onto the Lower Hawksbill Trail and follow it for 0.7 mile to the parking lot. The descent is steep and the going a bit slow for some.

Miles and Directions

0.0 Trailhead at north end of Hawksbill Gap parking lot. Access Appalachian Trail at the end of a 100-yard spur trail. Turn left.

0.4 First of three talus slopes, some views.

1.0 Cement post. Make hard left onto Salamander Trail.

1.9 Hawksbill summit and observation deck.

2.1 Cement post below and left of shelter. Turn left onto Lower Hawksbill Trail.

2.8 Return to trailhead.

13 Whiteoak Canyon

Start: From Mile 31.5 on Skyline Drive (Thornton Gap), take U.S. Highway 211 east to Sperryville. From there, continue to U.S. Highway 522 south. Go 0.8 mile, turn right onto Highway 231, and go about 9.5 miles to Secondary Road 643. Go south on SR 643 for about 10 miles to the junction with Secondary Road 600; turn right (west) onto SR 600 and stay on this road for 3.6 miles, to the point where the road fords Cedar Run. You will see the parking lot from here. The trailhead is at the far end.

Type of hike: Out and back.

Distance: 5.8 miles.

Approximate hiking time: 3 hours.

Elevation gain and loss: About 1,670 feet.

Maps: National Geographic Trails Illustrated Topo Map 228; Map 10, Appalachian Trail and other trails in Shenandoah National Park, Central District (PATC, Inc.).

The Hike

Although this hike is almost 6 miles long, we have included it here because there is so much to see along the way. The inbound portion of the hike is uphill, but at any time you can turn around and make the easy downhill hike back to the trailhead.

This hike provides access to some of the most spectacular falls in the park. The farther you go, the more falls you will pass—six if you complete the entire hike.

Begin your hike from the parking lot just off SR 600 and follow the Whiteoak Canyon Trail, which crosses Cedar Run almost immediately via a footbridge. After about 0.1 mile, a cement post indicates the junction with Cedar Run Trail from the left. Stay right on Whiteoak Canyon Trail. At

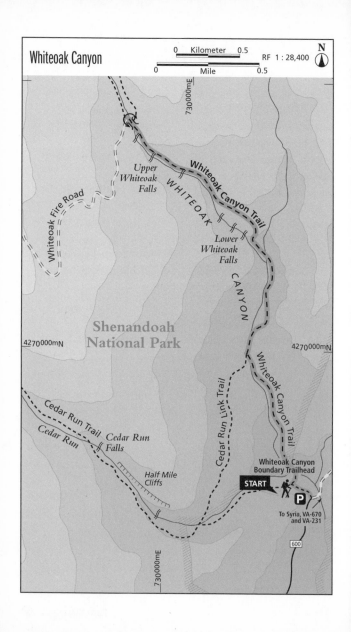

Whiteoak Canyon

0 Kilometer 0.5
0 Mile 0.5

RF 1 : 28,400

N

730000mE

Upper
Whiteoak
Falls

Whiteoak Canyon Trail

WHITEOAK

Whiteoak Fire Road

Lower
Whiteoak
Falls

CANYON

4270000mN

**Shenandoah
National Park**

4270000mN

Whiteoak Canyon Trail

Cedar Run Trail

Cedar Run

Cedar Run
Falls

Cedar Run Link Trail

Half Mile
Cliffs

Whiteoak Canyon
Boundary Trailhead

START

P

To Syria, VA-670
and VA-231

600

0.7 mile, continue to your right on the Whiteoak Canyon Trail. This is the junction with Cedar Run Link Trail, which leads to a part of Shenandoah that has been designated as wilderness.

The ascent of Whiteoak Canyon is steep and may require scrambling around numerous rocks. That is the bad news. The good news is that after hiking only a mile, there are great views of waterfalls and pools. If you take your time, stopping to snack, eat lunch, or dangle your feet in the water, you should be able to make it to the Whiteoak Falls overlook without too much effort.

The last falls are at 2.9 miles. The point is marked by a cement post. Simply turn around here and enjoy the views again as you make your way downhill and back to the parking lot.

Miles and Directions

0.0 From the parking lot, cross a footbridge and proceed along Whiteoak Canyon Trail.

0.1 Cement post designating intersection with Cedar Run Trail. Stay right on Whiteoak Canyon Trail.

0.7 Cedar Run Link Trail comes in from the left. Stay right on Whiteoak Canyon Trail.

1.5 Cement post at base of first falls. The trail swings to the right.

1.8 View of falls and pool from the rocks to the left of the trail.

2.7 Spur trail leads 0.1 mile to base of Whiteoak Falls.

2.9 Whiteoak Falls overlook on left. Retrace steps.

5.8 Return to parking lot.

14 **Dark Hollow Falls**

Start: Mile 50.7 on Skyline Drive.
Type of hike: Out and back.
Distance: 1.4 miles.
Approximate hiking time: 1.5 to 2 hours.

Elevation gain and loss: 440 feet.
Maps: National Geographic Trails Illustrated Topo Map 228; Map 10, Appalachian Trail and other trails in Shenandoah National Park, Central District (PATC, Inc.).

The Hike

The trail descends from the parking lot and follows Hogcamp Branch. At 0.6 mile, there is an overlook of 70-foot Dark Hollow Falls. The rails along the trail should not require a statement of intent but apparently do; invariably, some visitors fail to realize that the fences are intended not only to prevent further erosion but also to save life and limb. This is one place with a history of injury. Please remain on the trail! Rocks can be wet and very slippery.

Continue for another 0.1 mile to the base of Dark Hollow Falls. If you enjoy the spectacle, be aware that you are in good company. According to a resident naturalist, Thomas Jefferson also once appreciated this scene.

The falls are obviously appealing, especially if you consider their source. Hogcamp Branch drains the Big Meadow Swamp, which can be relatively dry during some of the summer. Nevertheless, Hogcamp manages to gather enough water in its progression toward Dark Hollow Falls to create a lovely falls. From here, you can descend farther to enjoy yet other falls created by Hogcamp Branch, or you can return to

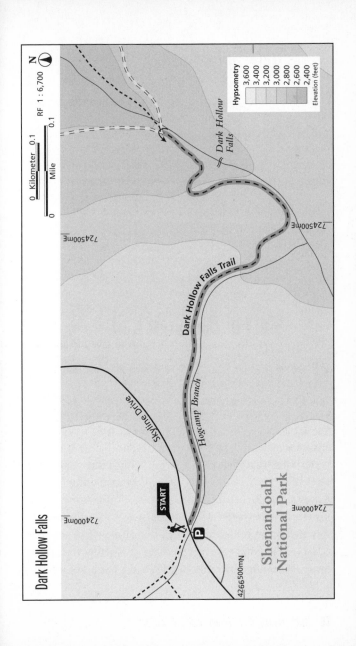

the trailhead. From the base of Dark Hollow Falls, climb 0.7 mile and about 440 feet in elevation to your starting point.

The descent to the falls is the easy part of the hike. A few benches have been placed along the trail to provide you with opportunities to rest on the return trip and to reflect on the area's scenic beauty.

Pets are not allowed on this trail.

Miles and Directions

0.0 Parking lot.

0.6 Overlook of Dark Hollow Falls.

0.7 Base of Dark Hollow Falls. Retrace your steps.

1.4 Return to parking lot.

15 Story of the Forest Trail

See map on page 54.
Start: Mile 51, across Skyline Drive from the north entrance of Byrd Visitor Center.
Type of hike: Loop.
Distance: 1.8 miles.
Approximate hiking time: 1 to 2 hours.

Elevation gain and loss: 290 feet.
Maps: National Geographic Trails Illustrated Topo Map 228; Map 10, Appalachian Trail and other trails in Shenandoah National Park, Central District (PATC, Inc.).

The Hike

This delightful, informative walk is a self-guided tour to the wonders of a Blue Ridge forest. It's a hike for everyone, especially children, as they will probably get good views of wildlife. Pets are not allowed on the trail.

At the trailhead, bear right (the maintenance area is to the left). You will be on a wide trail, which is gravel, forest floor, then paved.

This part of the hike is 0.8 mile long and is well marked. It is followed by a mile of paved biking and walking path leading back to the visitor center.

Miles and Directions

0.0   Trailhead. Stay on paved path to the right.

0.2   Bridge over Hogcamp Branch. Stay left at junction.

0.4   Junction with horse trail; keep going straight.

0.8   Big Meadows Campground. Turn left to access paved biking/walking path.

1.8   Return to trailhead.

16 Lewis Spring Falls

Start: Big Meadows Campground, Mile 51.2 on Skyline Drive.
Type of hike: Loop.
Distance: 3.3 miles.
Approximate hiking time: 3 to 4 hours.

Elevation gain and loss: 990 feet.
Maps: National Geographic Trails Illustrated Topo Map 228; Map 10, Appalachian Trail and other trails in Shenandoah National Park, Central District (PATC, Inc.).

The Hike

Walk to the amphitheater behind the picnic area. Take the Appalachian Trail south (left). Below the amphitheater, at the cement post, pick up the blue blazes of the Lewis Spring Falls Trail, which branches to the right. (If you want to stay

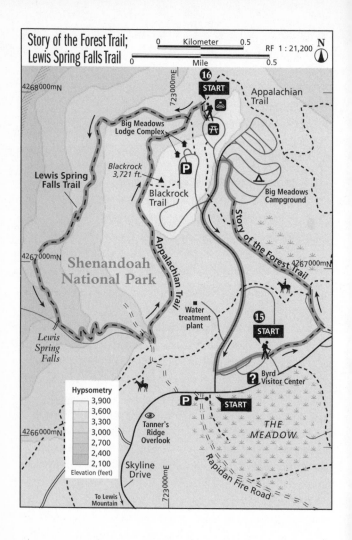

Story of the Forest Trail;
Lewis Spring Falls Trail

Kilometer   RF 1 : 21,200   N
0   0.5

Mile
0   0.5

16
START

Appalachian
Trail

4268000mN

Big Meadows
Lodge Complex

**Lewis Spring
Falls Trail**

*Blackrock
3,721 ft.*

P

Blackrock
Trail

Big Meadows
Campground

Story of the Forest Trail

4267000mN

**Shenandoah
National Park**

Appalachian Trail

4267000mN

*Lewis
Spring
Falls*

Water
treatment
plant

15
START

Byrd
Visitor Center

P   START

Hypsometry
3,900
3,600
3,300
3,000
2,700
2,400
2,100
Elevation (feet)

4266000mN

Tanner's
Ridge
Overlook

Skyline
Drive

*THE
MEADOW*

723000mE

Rapidan Fire Road

To Lewis
Mountain

on the AT, Milam Gap is 2.6 miles south; Fishers Gap is 1.6 miles north.)

This well-maintained trail descends immediately and continues to do so for about a mile. The rocky trail requires sturdy hiking boots. Watch yourself on the rocks—even dry ones can be slippery. Notice the many fallen trees, evidence of the power of ice and wind storms.

The path is flanked on both sides by hardwood trees and low-growth bushes. Descend into a hollow with some granite outcroppings. Stay alert for wildlife. Deer abound, and on our hike we ran into a member of a less-welcome species— one of the forest's spotted skunks, a unique member of the weasel family. Though the animal lifted its tail, it also lowered it as we backed off, so we carried no bad smell back to our tent.

When the trail finally levels, you can hear the falls; another brief ascent brings you to a nice overlook with views to the western mountains. Turn left, to the southeast, and follow the blue blazes to the observation point. Cross a small stream and parallel an iron railing. Do not attempt to climb down to the base of the falls. People have suffered serious, even fatal, falls trying this.

Lewis Spring Falls is the fourth highest falls in the park. It's a beautiful, gentle falls that cascades 81 feet. You can get a safe and commanding view of the falls from an overlook that was constructed by young men working in the Civilian Conservation Corps (CCC) camps in the 1930s.

From the overlook, backtrack north for about 50 feet and pick up the blue blazes going east. The trail maintains an uphill grade, sure and steady. It parallels a creek on your right and then switchbacks away from the stream.

After a climb of 0.6 mile, there is a cement marker. Go east for 70 yards on Lewis Spring Fire Road then turn north (left) onto the AT. Follow the white blazes on the trees. From this point (you are still chugging uphill), the Big Meadows Lodge is another 1.4 miles. The campground is half a mile beyond that.

Be sure to carry water on this hike. There are several signs cautioning hikers not to drink the water along the way. Some is "contaminated," say the signs, and requires "vigorous boiling." One common contaminant is *Giardia,* a waterborne parasite that can cause severe diarrhea, cramps, and fatigue. The parasite can survive in very cold water and is spread by the droppings of dogs, horses, cattle, elk, rabbits, and other small mammals, as well as humans.

Alternative hike: For families with children under the age of nine or ten, the above hike to Lewis Spring Falls may be too strenuous. A somewhat shorter, easier alternative is to descend a wide, gravel service road that is just south of the Big Meadows complex. Pass yellow-blazed horse trails to the left and right and come to a junction with the Appalachian Trail at 0.3 mile. Just past the junction, take the blue-blazed Lewis Spring Falls Trail on your left. Follow that for 0.6 mile to another junction. Here, take the spur trail to your left, which leads to a nice overlook near the top of the falls. Retrace your steps from this point, which will be mostly uphill.

This hike is 2 miles long and has an elevation gain and loss of about 800 feet. If you are hiking with young children, this may take two to three hours. Be sure to carry sufficient water.

Miles and Directions

0.0 Amphitheater behind picnic area at Big Meadows Campground. Access Appalachian Trail to the left, just off paved road.

0.1 Junction; take Lewis Spring Falls Trail (blue blazes) and begin descent (west and south).

1.0 View to west; turn south to overlook.

1.3 Falls observation point, 250 feet ahead. Backtrack to main trail.

1.9 Cement post. Go east 70 yards to access AT.

3.3 Back to campground.

17 Rapidan Camp (formerly called Camp Hoover)

Start: Parking lot at Milam Gap, Skyline Mile 52.8. Access the Appalachian Trail on the east side of Skyline Drive.
Type of hike: Out and back.
Distance: 4 miles.
Approximate hiking time: 2 to 3 hours.

Elevation gain and loss: About 850 feet.
Maps: National Geographic Trails Illustrated Topo Map 228; Map 10, Appalachian Trail and other trails in Shenandoah National Park, Central District (PATC, Inc.).

The Hike

The trail begins on the east side of the Milam Gap parking lot, just north of Milepost 53. To reach the trailhead, cross Skyline Drive to the side opposite the parking lot. From

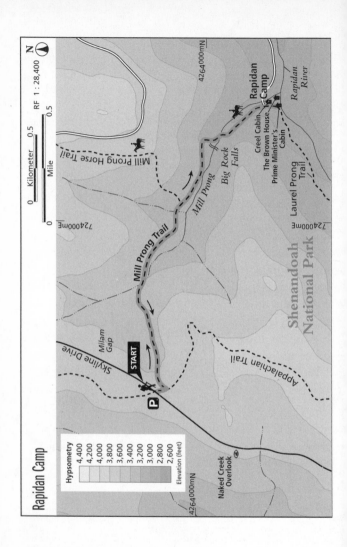

Rapidan Camp

N

RF 1 : 28,400

0   Kilometer   0.5

0   Mile   0.5

Mill Prong Horse Trail

Skyline Drive

Milam Gap

Mill Prong Trail

START

P

Mill Prong

Big Rock Falls

Mill Prong Trail

724000mE

4264000mN

Appalachian Trail

Shenandoah National Park

Laurel Prong Trail

Creel Cabin

The Brown House

Prime Minister's Cabin

Rapidan Camp

Rapidan River

724000mE

4264000mN

Naked Creek Overlook

Hypsometry

4,400
4,200
4,000
3,800
3,600
3,400
3,200
3,000
2,800
2,600

Elevation (feet)

here, follow the Appalachian Trail for a short distance until you reach its junction with Mill Prong Trail. Turn left onto Mill Prong Trail and begin a gradual descent, paralleling Mill Prong. A sign explains that fishing in the creek is permitted. However, "all fish must be handled carefully and returned immediately to the stream," and "only artificial flies or lures with a single hook are permitted."

After 1.5 miles, the trail passes Big Rock Falls. Continue following the trail downhill for a total of 2 miles, until you encounter a bridge crossing Mill Prong, which is almost immediately adjacent to the Rapidan River. Cross the bridge and climb the short bank to Rapidan Camp.

President Herbert Hoover came to Rapidan Camp for rest and relaxation. He was an avid outdoorsman and enjoyed fishing the many nearby creeks. Thirteen structures provided the backdrop for his vacations, which were often working vacations. Of the original thirteen only three remain: the Brown House (which has been fully restored, inside and out), the Creel Cabin, and the Prime Minister's Cabin. The setting is just as beautiful today as it was when Hoover retreated to Shenandoah. To him, the retreat met three key criteria: It was within 100 miles of Washington; it was located on a trout stream; and it was 2,500 feet above sea level. Because of the historic significance of the area, Congress has designated Rapidan Camp a historic landmark.

Laurel Prong and Mill Prong converge near the camp to create the Rapidan River. The river is full of deep pools that still contain trout like the ones that enticed President Hoover.

Miles and Directions

0.0   Milam Gap. Go about 40 yards on the Appalachian Trail. Turn left onto Mill Prong Trail.

0.7   Cross stream.

1.1   Cross stream.

1.5   Big Rock Falls.

2.0   Rapidan Camp. Retrace steps.

4.0   Return to Milam Gap.

18 Bearfence Mountain

Start: Bearfence Mountain parking lot, Skyline Mile 56.4. Cross to the east side of Skyline Drive. Access Bearfence Mountain Trail at cement post.
Type of hike: Loop.
Distance: 1.2 miles.
Approximate hiking time: 1 to 2 hours.

Elevation gain and loss: 380 feet.
Maps: National Geographic Trails Illustrated Topo Map 228; Map 10, Appalachian Trail and other trails in Shenandoah National Park, Central District (PATC, Inc.).

The Hike

Bearfence Mountain (3,640 feet) is one of several summits in the park that command a complete panoramic view: Massanutten Mountain and the Shenandoah Valley to the west and Laurel Gap, Fork Mountain, and Bluff Mountain to the east. In the short hike from the parking lot to the summit, you pass through the sandstone of the Swift Run Formation, capped by Catoctin basalt.

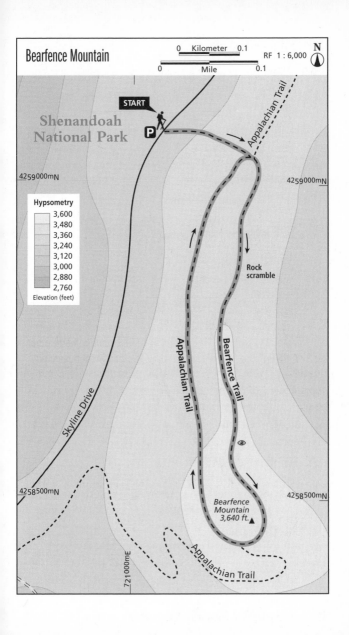

Bearfence Mountain

| | Kilometer | | RF 1 : 6,000 | N |
| 0 | | 0.1 | | |

| 0 | Mile | 0.1 |

START

Shenandoah
National Park

P

Appalachian Trail

4259000mN

4259000mN

Hypsometry

	3,600
	3,480
	3,360
	3,240
	3,120
	3,000
	2,880
	2,760

Elevation (feet)

Rock
scramble

Appalachian Trail

Bearfence Trail

Skyline Drive

Appalachian Trail

4258500mN

4258500mN

Bearfence
Mountain
3,640 ft. ▲

721000mE

Appalachian Trail

Hiking to the summit requires some degree of coordination. Though expertise in rock climbing is not necessary, you'll need some dexterity to maneuver through jumbled rocks. In some cases, you may find yourself scooting along on your bottom. To ensure good traction and to diminish the possibility of bruised feet, we recommend that you wear good hiking boots, although they won't help much if the rocks are wet or covered with snow. In summer, park officials have seen rattlesnakes in the area, so watch where you place your feet and hands. Park handouts indicate that this is not a trail for small children, especially those who must be carried. Pets are not allowed on this trail.

The hike to Bearfence begins at Mile 56.4 on the east side of Skyline Drive, across the road from the Bearfence Mountain parking lot. Almost immediately after leaving the parking lot, climb uphill. In several places, there are trees felled by the many severe storms since 1996. Their giant, exposed roots provide mute testimony to the humbling power of nature.

Within 300 yards of the parking lot, the trail begins to thread through huge boulders. This rock was originally volcanic lava, but with millions of years of compression, it has metamorphosed into the gray-green rock you see today. Appropriately, it is called greenstone, but only recent fractures reveal the green coloration.

If you are out of shape, it may seem as though the tortuous maze of boulders will never end, but the trail opens within a few hundred yards. You know you have reached the summit when you can peer down on everything. Looking east, you can see mountains ranging from Hazeltop to Kirtley. Looking west, you can see Skyline Drive, Shenandoah Valley, and Devils Tanyard. You are standing 3,640 feet above sea level.

From Bearfence Mountain, you can retrace your steps to the trailhead for a total hike of 0.8 mile, or you can continue toward the Appalachian Trail. At the cement post, take the AT north for about 0.7 mile back to the parking lot, for a trek of 1.2 miles.

Miles and Directions

0.0   Cement post, east side of Skyline Drive. Trail ascends (blue blazes).

0.1   Cross Appalachian Trail.

0.4   Bearfence summit.

0.5   AT junction; turn right and descend on AT.

1.2   Return to Bearfence Mountain parking lot.

19 Pocosin Trail

Start: About 50 yards down Pocosin Fire Road, on east side of Skyline Drive, Mile 59.5.
Type of hike: Out and back.
Distance: 2 miles.
Approximate hiking time: 1 to 2 hours.

Elevation gain and loss: 450 feet.
Maps: National Geographic Trails Illustrated Topo Map 228; Map 10, Appalachian Trail and other trails in Shenandoah National Park, Central District (PATC, Inc.).

The Hike

Locate the trailhead by driving first to Mile 59.5 on Skyline Drive. Then turn left onto Pocosin Fire Road on the east side of the drive. Park near the yellow chain and begin your hike down the fire road, which proceeds in an easterly

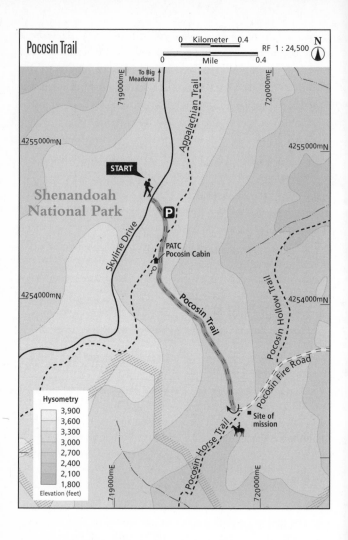

Pocosin Trail

RF 1 : 24,500

N

0   Kilometer   0.4

0   Mile   0.4

To Big
Meadows

719000mE

720000mE

4255000mN

Appalachian Trail

START

Shenandoah
National Park

P

Skyline Drive

PATC
Pocosin Cabin

Pocosin Trail

4254000mN

Pocosin Hollow Trail

Pocosin Fire Road

Hysometry

3,900
3,600
3,300
3,000
2,700
2,400
2,100
1,800
Elevation (feet)

Site of
mission

Pocosin Horse Trail

719000mE

720000mE

direction and crosses the Appalachian Trail at 0.1 mile. At 0.2 mile, it approaches the Pocosin Cabin, one in a chain of cabins that serves hikers using the AT. They are managed by the Potomac Appalachian Trail Club and are available for rent. To visit the cabin (if unoccupied), turn right onto the side path.

Continue along the fire road, which begins a slight descent. Throughout the spring and summer—and sometimes into the fall—wildflowers flank the trail. Look for columbine in the late spring and milkweed in the summer. The latter is associated with disturbed sites.

Soon the trail levels, and after about a mile you encounter a cement post on the right, indicating the Pocosin Horse Trail (yellow blazes). Turn right onto the Pocosin Horse Trail and look immediately to the left at what seems to be an old mountain cabin. This is actually part of the ruins of an Episcopal mission established here around 1904. Near the ruined cabin is all that remains of the old church—its stone steps.

Explore and let your imagination run loose. Story has it that in 1904 a young minister wanted to build an Episcopal mission in the dark, brooding hollow the locals then called the "Dark Pocosan." The locals violently opposed the mission, but rather than let that scare him off, the minister approached a local mountain man and said, "I hear you want to kill me." The mountain man was so impressed with the minister's bravery that the minister was able to build the new mission without incident. The church soon attracted residents of the Dark Pocosan (later Pocosin), who came to worship driving horse-drawn carriages and sometimes hiking the paths.

Though the forest is swallowing the artifacts of the period, a number of features from the mission days still remain. Old stone stairs and crumbling mission walls are among them. Hiking the several trails that take you to the old mission provides a rewarding excursion, but remember that old timbers and dilapidated rock walls attract snakes, so watch where you are going and where you put your hands.

Once you have finished exploring, retrace your steps.

Miles and Directions

0.0 Trailhead. Pass chain and follow yellow-blazed Pocosin Fire Road.

0.1 Cement post. Stay on fire road as it crosses Appalachian Trail.

0.2 Cement post. Stay on fire road. PATC Pocosin Cabin (locked) to right.

0.9 Cement post on right and junction with Pocosin Horse Trail and Pocosin Hollow Trail to left. Turn right onto Pocosin Horse Trail and follow yellow blazes.

1.0 Ruins of Episcopal mission on left. Retrace steps.

2.0 Return to trailhead.

20 South River Falls

Start: South River picnic area, Mile 62.8 on Skyline Drive.
Type of hike: Out and back.
Distance: 4.4 miles.
Approximate hiking time: 2 to 3 hours.

Elevation gain and loss: 800 feet.
Maps: National Geographic Trails Illustrated Topo Map 228; Map 10, Appalachian Trail and other trails in Shenandoah National Park, Central District (PATC, Inc.).

The Hike

The trailhead to South River Falls is to the right of the drinking fountain at the picnic grounds, at Mile 62.8 on Skyline Drive. The trail descends gradually for 0.1 mile to a junction with the Appalachian Trail. A cement post orients you to the surrounding features. Milam Gap and Swift Run Gap are 11.5 miles and 3 miles to the southwest, respectively.

Continue your hike from the post following the blue balzes, and begin a series of gradual switchbacks as you descend the trail. In places the trail is rocky, but it is wide and, for the most part, smooth until it approaches the first of several creeks that combine to create South River. In the past, hikers have attempted to save time by cutting across the trail, creating erosion. As a result, the park stipulates via several signs that hikers remain on the trail.

At 0.75 mile, you will encounter another creek entering from the left. It is difficult to see, because it runs beneath the rocks, but it certainly is audible. Just past the creek are a number of trees downed by the strong winds of

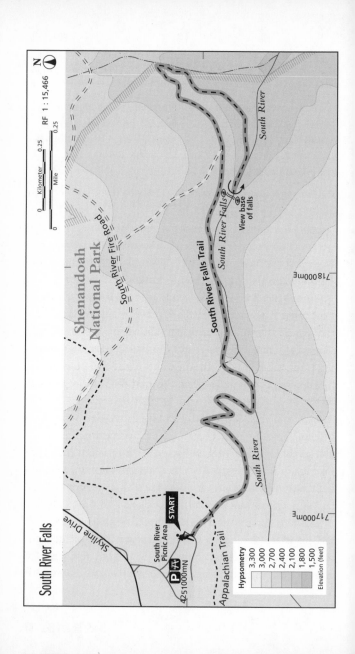

South River Falls

a September 1996 storm. Other creeks continue to flow from the left into the South River, which parallels the trail as it continues its descent.

Just a few yards past the juncture of the creek, the South River plunges dramatically downward into a great hollow. It is difficult to see the falls until you approach a natural overlook, located 1.3 miles from the trailhead. Do not get too close to the edge. A few yards farther along the trail, cement walls provide a more protected spot from which to view the falls below you.

At this point, you may turn around and retrace your steps, making this a 2.6-mile hike. If you have the time and energy, continue on to the base of the falls for a journey of 4.4 miles.

If you continue, the trail joins an old road that comes in from the left in 0.2 mile. It leads to the South River Falls Fire Road. However, continue along the widening South River Falls Trail, which was once used by inhabitants traveling from one hollow to another. This wider trail descends for 0.6 mile and then swings back toward the base of the falls and a cement post encircled by an aluminum band. The post states that it is 0.3 mile to the end of the road and the park's boundary with the Virginia Wildlife Management Area. It also advises you of the existence of a short spur trail to the fall's base about 0.1 mile away. Take the narrow spur trail. You may have to scurry over downed trees.

At 83 feet, South River Falls is the park's third largest falls. A refreshing pool at its base would be invigorating on a hot summer day—all the better to prepare you for the challenging hike back up to the trailhead.

Miles and Directions

0.0   Trailhead located past drinking fountain at South River picnic area; descend.

0.1   Cross Appalachian Trail and continue descent on South River Falls Trail following the blue blazes.

1.3   Overlook for South River Falls.

1.5   Junction with old road.

2.1   Path from trail to spur trail.

2.2   Spur trail to South River Falls. Retrace route.

4.4   Trailhead; end of hike.

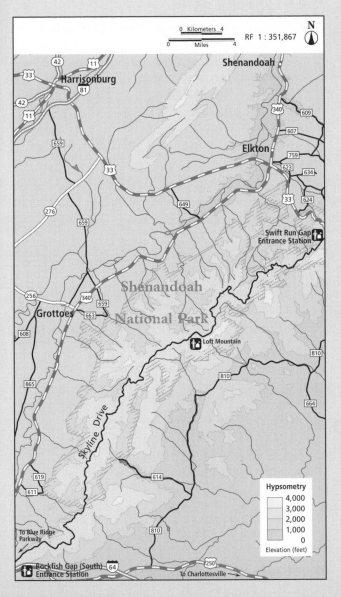

21 Powell Gap

Start: Mile 70 on Skyline Drive, at sign for Powell Gap. Park along east side of road near small meadow.
Type of hike: Out and back.
Distance: 1 mile.
Approximate hiking time: 30 to 60 minutes.

Elevation gain and loss: 300 to 400 feet.
Maps: National Geographic Trails Illustrated Topo Map 228; Map 11, Appalachian Trail and other trails in Shenandoah National Park, South District (PATC, Inc.).

The Hike

Access the trail by walking to the cement post adjacent to the POWELL GAP sign. This hike follows the Appalachian Trail south. Immediately, it begins to climb, gradually but steadily; it peaks at a short spur trail that provides an overlook to the east. After soaking in the countryside and, if you are lucky, some sun, return to your vehicle.

On a late fall or early winter day, this hike could lead to some spectacular views. This is one of our favorite short hikes.

Miles and Directions

0.0 Cement post on east side of Skyline Drive. Follow Appalachian Trail south.
0.5 Rock ledge. Retrace steps.
1.0 Cement post; end of hike.

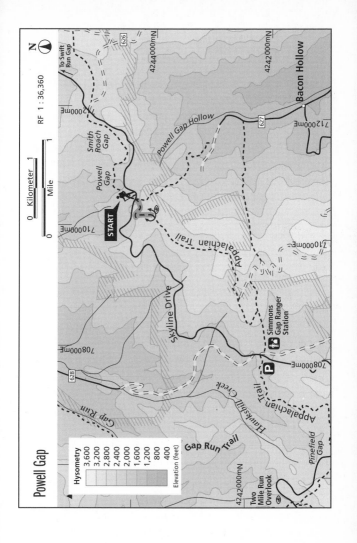

Powell Gap

22 Ivy Creek

Start: Ivy Creek Overlook, Skyline Drive, Mile 77.5. Access the Appalachian Trail from south end of parking lot at cement post (white blazes).
Type of hike: Out and back.
Distance: 2.8 miles.
Approximate hiking time: 2 to 3 hours.

Elevation loss and gain: 695 feet.
Maps: National Geographic Trails Illustrated Topo Map 228; Map 11, Appalachian Trail and other trails in Shenandoah National Park, South District (PATC, Inc.).

The Hike

The hike begins on the south side of the Ivy Creek Overlook. Turn south onto the Appalachian Trail and begin a gradual descent amid sassafras, laurel, oak, and pine. The trail then begins to climb and makes several switchbacks, passing by several large boulders. Soon, there will be beautiful views to the east of Loft Mountain. In late summer, the trail is flanked by mint, goldenrod, and yellow daisies. In winter the trail is open and spacious and provides seemingly unending views.

At 0.7 mile, the trail reaches an opening on the right from which you can see Skyline Drive and Patterson Ridge below. This is a good place to turn around if you are tired or time is short. If you choose to continue, start downhill amid blueberries—a species popular with the bears.

As the trail continues its descent, Ivy Creek is on the left. At 1.4 miles, there is a creek and a beautiful, small pool—a nice spot to rest and snack. This is the only place in the park where the AT parallels a stream for any considerable distance. Enjoy, and then return the way you came.

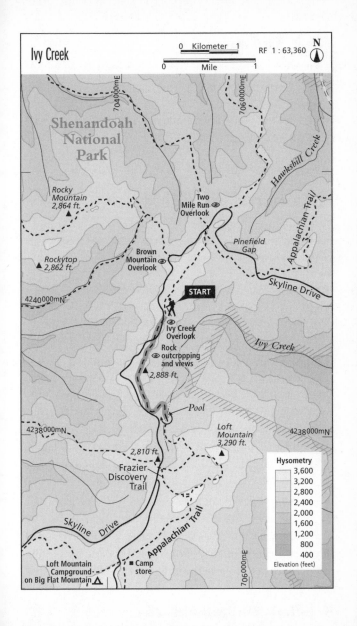

Miles and Directions

0.0 Ivy Creek Overlook, Mile 77.5 on Skyline Drive. Turn south onto Appalachian Trail.

0.7 Rock outcropping.

1.4 Ivy Creek and pool. Retrace steps.

2.8 Return to Ivy Creek Overlook.

23 Loft Mountain Loop

Start: Loft Mountain Wayside parking lot on Skyline Drive, Mile 79.5.
Type of hike: Loop.
Distance: 2.7 miles.
Approximate hiking time: 2 hours.

Elevation gain and loss: About 600 feet.
Maps: National Geographic Trails Illustrated Topo Map 228; Map 11, Appalachian Trail and other trails in Shenandoah National Park, South District (PATC, Inc.).

The Hike

From the wayside parking lot, walk north on Skyline Drive for about 150 yards. Pass the trailhead for the Patterson Ridge Trail (a one-way trail) on the left. Turn right onto the first dirt road, and proceed to the Ivy Creek PATC Maintenance Building and the Ivy Creek Spring. A junction with the Appalachian Trail is about 200 yards ahead. Upon reaching it, turn right and ascend through hardwood forest.

As you approach the summit of Loft Mountain, the trees grow more sparsely and blackberry bushes abound. After about a mile, the trail levels out on the ridgetop and continues to an overlook with rock outcroppings on the left side

Loft Mountain Loop

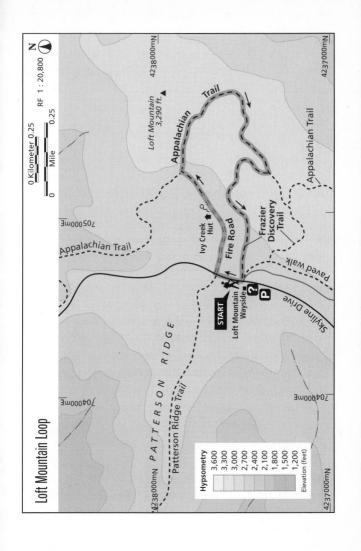

- Hypsometry
- 3,600
- 3,300
- 3,000
- 2,700
- 2,400
- 2,100
- 1,800
- 1,500
- 1,200

Elevation (feet)

N

RF 1 : 20,800

0 Kilometer 0.25

0 Mile 0.25

PATTERSON RIDGE

Patterson Ridge Trail

Appalachian Trail

Loft Mountain 3,290 ft.

Appalachian Trail

Ivy Creek Hut

Fire Road

Frazier Discovery Trail

Appalachian Trail

START

Loft Mountain Wayside

P

?

Skyline Drive

Paved walk

4238000mN

705000mE

4238000mN

704000mE

4237000mN

4237000mN

of the trail. From here you get a lovely 180-degree view to the east of the Piedmont (on clear days); to the left is Flattop Mountain, and to the right is Fox Mountain with three peaks, a hollow, then two more peaks. The valley below is pastoral, and you can watch clouds and storms roll in. Also along the ridgetop are fields of yarrow and more berry bushes.

At the next cement post, you have several options. We turned right onto the Frazier Discovery Trail and encountered another great viewpoint on the right. You can follow the trail down to Skyline Drive and the wayside parking lot.

This is a very enjoyable hike and one that is suitable for the whole family. Pets are not allowed on the Frazier Discovery Trail.

Miles and Directions

0.0   Loft Mountain Wayside parking lot. Follow Skyline Drive north for 150 yards to dirt fire road on right.

60 yds.   Cement post on right. Turn right onto dirt road; ascend.

0.4   Cement post, Ivy Creek PATC Maintenance Building and spring. Follow blue blazes uphill. Cross small creek.

0.6   Cement post; junction with Appalachian Trail. Turn right onto AT and follow white blazes uphill.

1.0   Trail levels on ridgetop.

1.1   Overlook on left.

1.4   Cement post. Turn right onto Frazier Discovery Trail.

1.5   Side trail to right leading to overlook. Follow the Frazier Discovery Trail for another 1.2 miles down to the trailhead on Skyline Drive.

2.7   Trailhead; end of hike.

24 Blackrock Summit

Start: Skyline Mile 84.8, at Blackrock parking lot on west side of Skyline Drive.
Type of hike: Loop.
Distance: 1 mile.
Approximate hiking time: 30 to 60 minutes.

Elevation gain and loss: 175 feet.
Maps: National Geographic Trails Illustrated Topo Map 228; Map 11, Appalachian Trail and other trails in Shenandoah National Park, South District (PATC, Inc.).

The Hike

The trailhead is located at a sign in the Blackrock parking lot that interprets the mountain's geology. After reading it, ascend rather sharply for 0.1 mile on the Trayfoot Mountain Trail to its junction with the Appalachian Trail. Take the AT south (left), following the white blazes. The AT remains level almost all the way to the summit—a distance from the junction of about 0.4 mile.

The trail stops just short of the summit. To reach it, you must scramble a short distance over a jumble of boulders, but the view makes the climb worth it. Occasionally, hikers report seeing rattlesnakes sunning themselves on the rocks, so watch where you step!

From the summit you can see Buzzard Rock and Trayfoot, Horsehead, and Furnace Mountains. On a very clear day, try to locate Hightop Mountain. From the summit you can take an easy trail to Trayfoot Summit, another 0.7 mile away, where there are the remains of an old fire tower, but you won't get any good views.

Blackrock Summit played an unusual role in Virginia history. During the Revolutionary War, Virginia governor

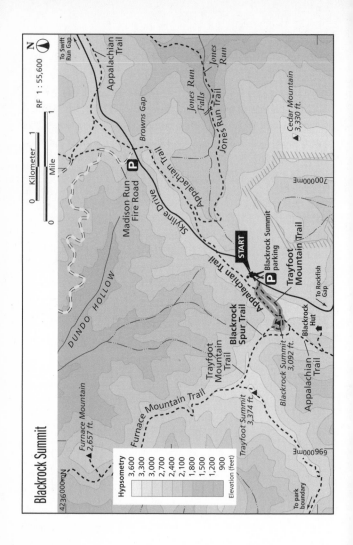

Blackrock Summit

Thomas Jefferson was reportedly concerned about the safety of the Great Seal of Virginia and the state archives. He gave them to a friend, who hid them in a cave at Blackrock until the war's end.

The hike continues, following the AT south around Blackrock Summit to another cement post. On the post, an arrow points left to the old road that is now part of Trayfoot Mountain Trail, and that leads back to the trailhead.

This a great hike for families.

Miles and Directions

0.0 Blackrock parking lot; ascend on Trayfoot Mountain Trail.

0.1 Intersection with Appalachian Trail; take AT south (white blazes).

0.5 Blackrock Summit.

0.6 Intersection of AT and Trayfoot Mountain Trail. Follow Trayfoot (blue blazes) back to trailhead.

1.0 Trailhead.

25 Calvary and Chimney Rocks

Start: Riprap parking lot on west side of Skyline Drive, Mile 90.
Type of hike: Out and back.
Distance: 3.2 miles.
Approximate hiking time: 2 to 3 hours.

Elevation gain and loss: About 850 feet.
Maps: National Geographic Trails Illustrated Topo Map 228; Map 11, Appalachian Trail and other trails in Shenandoah National Park, South District (PATC, Inc.).

The Hike

This 3.2-mile hike is moderately easy and one of the prettiest hikes in the park. Much of it is through a designated wilderness area.

From the end of the Riprap parking lot, take the Appalachian Trail north and follow the white blazes. Climb for 0.4 mile under a canopy of oak, maple, and sassafras, before reaching a cement post at the junction with the Riprap Trail. Go west (left), following the blue blazes. Now the trail is lined with blueberry bushes. It heads downhill via switchbacks and then climbs to a knoll jumbled with lichen-covered rocks and boulders—a jumble known as riprap.

At 0.7 mile you reach a saddle, from which you have great views of Paine Run Watershed. The striated boulders are Erwin quartzite, as are the rocks at Calvary Rocks and Chimney Rock, not far ahead. Follow the ridgetop up and down for 0.7 mile to Calvary Rocks, which offer a good northwest view. Continue another 0.2 mile to Chimney Rock. Iron pegs imbedded in the rock are part of an old bridge. Again, you have a good view to the west.

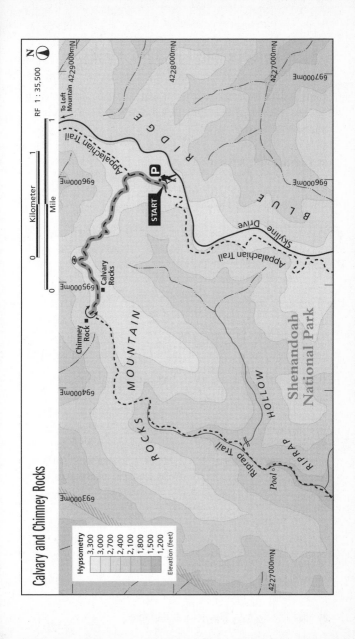

Calvary and Chimney Rocks

N

RF 1 : 35,500

Hypsometry
3,300
3,000
2,700
2,400
2,100
1,800
1,500
1,200
Elevation (feet)

Kilometer

Mile

To Loft
Mountain 4229000mN

Appalachian Trail

696000mE

P

START

BLUE RIDGE

Appalachian Trail

Skyline Drive

695000mE

Calvary Rocks

Chimney Rock

ROCKS MOUNTAIN

HOLLOW

RIPRAP

Riprap Trail

Pool

Shenandoah
National Park

694000mE

693000mE

4228000mN

697000mE

696000mE

4227000mN

From this point, you should retrace your steps to the Riprap parking lot. After Chimney Rock, the narrow trail levels, and there are a couple more small lookout points. Then it begins a gentle descent off the ridge and back into the forest before descending steeply for several more miles to the park boundary.

Miles and Directions

0.0 Cement post at Riprap parking lot.

0.4 Cement post. Go west, following blue blazes.

0.7 Talus slope.

1.4 Calvary Rocks.

1.6 Chimney Rock. Retrace steps.

3.2 Return to Riprap parking lot.

26 Calf Mountain

Start: Beagle Gap parking area on east side of Skyline Drive, Mile 99.5.
Type of hike: Out and back.
Distance: 2 miles.
Approximate hiking time: 1 to 2 hours.

Elevation gain and loss: 443 feet.
Maps: National Geographic Trails Illustrated Topo Map 228; Map 11, Appalachian Trail and other trails in Shenandoah National Park, South District (PATC, Inc.).

The Hike

This short climb up Calf Mountain is delightful, partly because the trail winds through old meadows rather than through woods, giving you a chance to see more of the

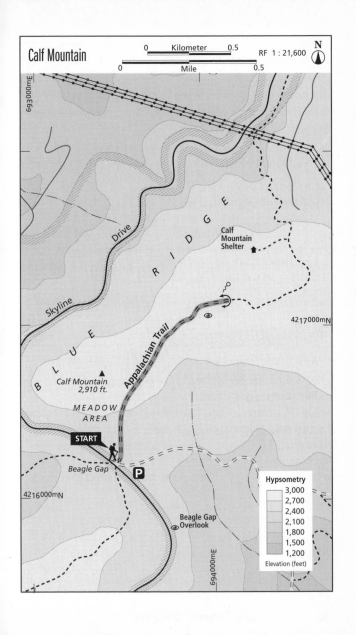

Calf Mountain

Kilometer	
0	0.5

RF 1 : 21,600

N

Mile	
0	0.5

693000mE

Drive

Skyline

R I D G E

Calf
Mountain
Shelter

4217000mN

B L U E

▲ Calf Mountain
2,910 ft.

Appalachian Trail

MEADOW
AREA

START

Beagle Gap

P

4216000mN

Beagle Gap
Overlook

694000mE

Hypsometry

	3,000
	2,700
	2,400
	2,100
	1,800
	1,500
	1,200

Elevation (feet)

landscape. The trail is dirt and well maintained. In summer, if it is hot and humid, you might want to hike this one early or late in the day.

Walk through the "V" opening in the wire fence and ascend through a meadow filled with wildflowers and berry bushes to the Appalachian Trail going north, which enters a small stand of new-growth trees and bushes and quickly gets steeper. Then it levels out and leads through meadows to a large stand of old but still-bearing apple trees—the remnants of an introduced apple orchard.

At 0.7 mile there is a good view to the east. You are not at the summit yet; the top is 0.3 mile farther. You will know you've reached the top if you begin to descend on logs and rocks placed across the trail. From the summit, you can wander on as far as time allows and then retrace your route to enjoy, once again, the area's openness and lush vegetation.

Miles and Directions

0.0 Beagle Gap parking lot. Walk through "V" opening in wire fence with white blaze on it.

0.7 View.

1.0 Summit of Calf Mountain. Retrace steps.

2.0 Return to Beagle Gap parking lot.

About the Authors

Bert Gildart has been writing about the outdoors for more than twenty years. For thirteen summers he served as a backcountry ranger in Glacier National Park. He has written more than 300 magazine articles for such publications as *Smithsonian, Travel & Leisure, Modern Maturity, Field & Stream,* and *National Wildlife.* Together, Bert and his wife, Jane, have hiked hundreds of miles throughout many wilderness and backcountry areas of the country. They have collaborated on several other FalconGuides including: *Hiking Shenandoah National Park, A FalconGuide to Death Valley National Park, A FalconGuide to Dinosaur National Monument, Best Easy Day Hikes Black Hills Country,* and *Hiking the Black Hills Country.*

Outfit
Your Mind

falcon.com

log in

learn more